BLUE FUNNEL

THE LATER YEARS

1925-1982

Compiled by
C. H. MILSOM

A *Sea Breezes* Publication

Units 28-30, Spring Valley Industrial Estate,
Braddan, Isle of Man IM2 2QS.

Always to be best, and distinguished above the rest.
— Homer's *Iliad*

The Captains and the Kings Depart

WHEN Alfred Holt and his brother Philip founded the Ocean Steam Ship Company in 1865 for the purpose of trading to China they regarded it as the greatest adventure of their lives and because the *Odyssey* was for them the finest adventure story ever written they gave Homeric names to their ships. Over the next 100 years the names of these mythological heroes became familiar in waters far removed from their native Greece and even now when they are gone their memory lives on, the ships themselves becoming legends in their own right.

A brief history of Alfred Holt & Company was given in *Blue Funnels in the Mersey* published by *Sea Breezes* in March, 1988, and only a summary is needed here to explain why some of the ships changed their names and/ or livery during their lives as Blue Funnel ships. The first complication came about in 1891 when a Dutch subsidiary was formed under the name Nederlandsche Stoomvaart Maatschappij "Oceaan". In 1902 a former competitor in the China trade, the China Mutual Steam Navigation Company, was purchased and thereafter the ships of what had become generally known as the Blue Funnel Line were distributed between Ocean Steam, China Mutual and NSM "Oceaan". Prior to 1972 ships owned by Ocean Steam and China Mutual were managed by Alfred Holt & Company but in that year the Ocean Steam Ship Company changed its name to Ocean Transport & Trading plc and the ships were owned by China Mutual with management by Blue Funnel Line Ltd.

The Glen Line, which incorporated the Shire Line, was acquired in 1935. Their ships carried the names of Scottish glens or Welsh counties but transfers between the lines were effected simply by changing the name and painting the funnel Glen Line red instead of Blue Funnel blue, or *vice versa*. The final complication came with the full acquisition of Elder Dempster Lines in 1967. This company had been associated with Alfred Holts since 1936 but there was no interchange of ships until the early 1970s when containerisation of the Far East trade made many of the conventional general cargo liners surplus to requirements. Most were scrapped but some were transferred to Elder Dempster's West African trade as the occasion warranted, often without change of name and only a perfunctory alteration to the livery.

The question will often be asked: Which was the last Blue Funnel ship? Ocean Transport & Trading claim that the distinction belongs to the *Barber Perseus* which was handed over to new owners on December 22, 1988, their criteria being that she had a blue funnel, carried a traditional Blue Funnel name and served in a traditional Blue Funnel trade. To my mind, however, the *Barber Perseus* fails on account of her name for no hero of Greek mythology carried the prefix "Barber" which is derived from the associated company Barber Line, of Oslo.

I prefer to think that the truly last Blue Funnel ships were the last pictured in this album. They were followed by a number of ships which sported a blue funnel well aft on their superstructure and carried names taken from Greek mythology but they carried oil, grain and other bulk cargoes and were operated by companies with strange names over routes which bore no resemblance to traditional Blue Funnel trades. They no doubt had their place but it is doubtful if they will be remembered with the same affection as the ships pictured in this album.

There remains, however, one other, the *Nestor,* 78,951 grt, which has a blue funnel and bears a name once revered throughout the fleet. Built in France in 1977 for the carriage of liquified natural gas she has been laid-up ever since in Loch Striven but should she ever sail in anything resembling a traditional trade she may yet become the very last Blue Funnel ship.

Many people have assisted in the preparation of this album but most of all I must thank David Keen, Keith P. Lewis and Charles Medcalf, all of Wirral, Merseyside, for their help in researching ship histories. I am also indebted for invaluable snippets of information from D. H. Johnzon, of Filey, Yorkshire; W. A. Mulhearn, of Pleasanton, California; Peter S. Staughton, of Warrandyte, Australia; and Julian Williams, of Hong Kong.

Between us we have consulted innumerable editions of *Lloyd's Register of Shipping, The Liberty Ships* by L. A. Sawyer and W. H. Mitchell (David & Charles, 1970), *Great Passenger Ships of the World* by Arnold Kludas (Patrick Stephens Ltd, 1976 and 1984), *British Merchant Vessels Lost or Damaged by Enemy Action During the Second World War* (HMSO, 1947), *A Merchant Fleet in War, 1939-1945* by Captain S. W. Roskill (Collins, 1962) and Alfred Holt & Company's staff magazines. All else has been taken from various editions of *Sea Breezes.*

Finally I must add an apology and a note of warning. The main aim of this album has been to present photographs of Blue Funnel ships as we who sailed in them knew them. After they left the service of Alfred Holt & Company many of those which were not sold for scrap disappeared into ownership and management of bewildering complexity, sailed under flags which bore little relationship to the nationality of their owners and changed their names so often and so rapidly that while every care has been taken in describing their subsequent histories it would be a braver man than I who would dare to claim total accuracy.

C. H. MILSOM

INDEX
of Blue Funnel Ships

The ships are shown in the order of the year in which they are believed to have entered service with Alfred Holt & Company with a blue funnel, but not necessarily according to the month of the year.

PHRONTIS
6,636 grt
1925: Caledon Shipbuilding & Engineering Co, Dundee, for NSM "Oceaan".
1940: Escaped from Amsterdam on May 12 as German forces invaded Holland. Embarked some 840 German prisoners-of-war at Ymuiden and 56 Dutch naval ratings to guard them and arrived at Dover on May 14.
1958: Sold in June to M.A. Bakhashab, of Jeddah; for £60,000 and renamed *Ryad;* arrived at Hong Kong in the following August to be broken up.

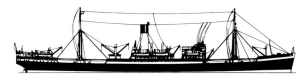

The "Orestes" and others of her class were the first ships in the Holt fleet to be fitted with electric cargo winches. An earlier "Orestes" opened the first direct Holt service between the UK and Australia in 1901

ORESTES
7,845 grt
1926: Workman, Clark & Co, Belfast, for the Ocean Steam Ship Co.
1942: Attacked by Japanese aircraft on April 2 off Madras but escaped serious damage. Attacked by surfaced Japanese submarine on June 9 off Sydney but again escaped serious damage.
1963: Sold in August to Nichimen Co Ltd, Osaka, Japan, for £84,500 for scrap and broken up at Mihara.

IDOMENEUS
7,847 grt
1926: Workman, Clark & Co, Belfast, for the China Mutual Steam Navigation Co.
1943: Fired on by submarine on May 7 off Sierra Leone and took swift avoiding action. The torpedoes missed and sank a ship in the next line of the convoy.
1945: Served as a victualling supply ship with the East Indies Fleet.
1962: Sold in April to Azienoa Recuperi Demolizioni Maritima, Genoa, for £90,000 for scrap.

The "Stentor" and her near sisters "Alcinous" and "Phrontis" were the precursors of the "engines aft" design devised by Alfred Holt & Co for the carriage of tobacco leaf and other uniform bulk cargoes. She was the first ship in the fleet to be fitted with a double-acting oil engine

STENTOR
6,626 grt
1926: Caledon Shipbuilding & Engineering Co, Dundee, for the China Mutual Steam Navigation Co.
1933: In collision with the *Guildford Castle* in the River Elbe on May 31, as a result of which the *Guildford Castle* sank. Court ruled both ships equally to blame.
1939: Joined in the first westbound convoy to sail through the Mediterranean and collided on September 16 with another ship, the *Dilwara*. Neither ship was seriously damaged and neither was found to blame for an incident which was considered an acceptable risk of sailing in convoy.
1941: Bombed and machine-gunned by British aircraft on April 3 at Jeddah. Her master demanded protection from a British destroyer against the activities of "friendly aircraft".
1942: Torpedoed on October 27 in position 29°13′N, 20°53′W (North Atlantic, west of Canary Islands) and sank in seven to eight minutes with the loss of 45 passengers and crew; 202 survivors were picked up by HMS *Woodruff.*

EURYBATES
6,443 grt
1928: Scotts' Shipbuilding & Engineering Co, Greenock, for the Ocean Steam Ship Co.
1951: Engines changed from part steam, part oil (Scott-Still) to oil only.
1958: Sold for scrap in July to Establissements Van Heyghen Freres for breaking up at Ghent.

AGAMEMNON
7,857 grt
1929: Workman Clark (1928) Ltd, Belfast, for the Ocean Steam Ship Co.
1939: Taken over by the Admiralty in December and converted to a minelayer (HMS *Agamemnon,* 1st Minelaying Squadron).
1943: On the 1st Minelaying Squadron being disbanded in the autumn, went to Vancouver for conversion into an amenities and recreation ship for use in Far East waters but the war ended before the work had been completed.
1947: Reverted to commercial service.
1963: Sold for scrap in March to Peninsular Shipping Enterprise Ltd, Hong Kong, for £89,700.

MENESTHEUS
7,771 grt
1929: Caledon Shipbuilding & Engineering Co, Dundee, for the Ocean Steam Ship Co.
1940: Taken over by the Admiralty and converted into a minelayer (HMS *Menestheus,* 1st Minelaying Squadron).
1942: Attacked by German aircraft off Iceland and hit by two bombs which failed to explode but which caused the bed of the engines to shift. Taken in tow by HMS *Agamemnon* to Lochalsh for repair.
1943: On the 1st Minelaying Squadron being disbanded in the autumn went to Vancouver for conversion into an amenities and recreation ship for use in Far East waters, the work including the addition of a dummy funnel. Joined the British Pacific Fleet after the war had ended.
1948: Returned to commercial service with one funnel.
1953: Suffered an engine-room explosion on April 16 off the coast of California, caught fire and had to be abandoned. Arrived under tow at Long Beach on May 5 and was sold in June to the Boston Iron & Metal Co for breaking-up at Baltimore.

HMS "Menestheus" at Malta in her guise as an amenities ship

MARON
6,487 grt
1930: Caledon Shipbuilding & Engineering Co, Dundee, for the China Mutual Steam Navigation Co.
1937: Requisitioned in August at Hong Kong to take 1,100 officers and men of the Royal Welch Fusiliers to Shanghai and returned with British evacuees.
1939: Requisitioned by the Admiralty.
1942: Torpedoed on November 13 in position 36°27′N, 00°58′W (Mediterranean, off Oran) and sank in less than 15 minutes. All the crew were picked up by HMS *Marigold* and landed at Gibraltar the next day.

CLYTONEUS
6,278 grt
1930: Scotts' Shipbuilding & Engineering Co, Greenock, for the Ocean Steam Ship Co.
1941: Bombed and sunk on January 8 in position 56°23′N, 15°28′W (280 miles north-west of Bloody Foreland) without loss of life. Two boatloads of survivors were rescued the next day by HMS *Wild Swan* and a third boatload by the armed merchant cruiser *Esperance Bay*.

MYRMIDON
6,278 grt
1930: Scotts' Shipbuilding & Engineering Co, Greenock, for the Ocean Steam Ship Co.
1941: While lying at Henderson's Wharf, Birkenhead, during an air raid on March 13 a bomb exploded on the quay nearby. The ship was hauled off but while crossing the dock she detonated an acoustic mine, the resulting damage causing her to settle on the bottom. After being raised and repaired she sailed on June 5 only to set off a magnetic mine in the River Mersey. Following further repairs she sailed again and was machine-gunned by aircraft off the Butt of Lewis in December, this time without suffering serious damage.
1942: Torpedoed on September 5 in position 00°45′N, 06°27′W (Gulf of Guinea). All 116 crew and 129 passengers were picked up by HMS *Brilliant* within a matter of hours.

POLYPHEMUS
6,269 grt
1930: Scotts' Shipbuilding & Engineering Co, Greenock, for NSM "Oceaan".
1942: On May 25 rescued 14 survivors from the Norwegian tanker *Norland* who had been adrift for five days after the torpedoing of their ship. Torpedoed herself the next day in a position 340 miles north of Bermuda and sank with the loss of 15 Chinese crew members. Of the five boats which got away, three were picked up off Nantucket Island and the other two by Portuguese ships, all within a week.

DEUCALION
7,516 grt
1930: Hawthorn, Leslie & Co, Newcastle, for the Ocean Ship Co.
1942: Bombed and afterwards torpedoed on August 12 while on passage to Malta with urgently needed supplies for the relief of the island (Operation Pedestal) and sank in position 37°56′N, 08°40′E (five miles west of Cani Rocks, Galita Island, off the coast of Tunisia). The survivors were picked up by HMS *Bramham* and some were later transferred to the tanker *Ohio* to strengthen and relieve the exhausted crew of that gallant vessel.

The oil engines of the "Ajax", built by Burmeister & Wain, of Copenhagen, were supercharged by the Buchi and Rateau system which raised the brake horsepower from 6,600 to 8,600 and as high as 10,000 on test

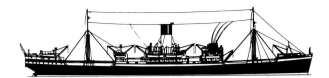

AJAX
7,540 grt
1931: Scotts' Shipbuilding & Engineering Co, Greenock, for the Ocean Steam Ship Co.
1957: Transferred in July to the Glen Line and renamed *Glenlochy*.
1958: Transferred in November to Ocean Steam Ship Co and renamed *Sarpedon*.
1962: Sold in November to Shiu Wing Co for £97,500 for scrap and broken up at Hong Kong.

MEMNON
7,506 grt
1931: Caledon Shipbuilding & Engineering Co, Dundee, for the China Mutual Steam Navigation Co.
1941: Torpedoed on March 11 in position 20°41′N, 21°00′W (Atlantic Ocean, 200 miles west of Cape Blanco) and sank with the loss of four lives. Two lifeboats got away, No 1 with 22 men and No 5 with 44 men. An attempt to even out the numbers was unsuccessful in the rough seas prevailing but on the following day four men and some stores were transferred from No 5 to No 1. Boat No 1 reached land at Yoff, near Dakar, on March 21. Boat No 5 was re-victualled by the French steamer *Kilissi* on March 21 and sailed on to Bathurst.

The last moments of the "Memnon"

GORGON
3,533 grt
1933: Caledon Shipbuilding & Engineering Co, Dundee, for joint ownership by the Ocean Steam Ship Co and the West Australian Steam Navigation Co.
1936: Became wholly owned by the Ocean Steam Ship Co on the withdrawal of the West Australian Steam Navigation Co from the Singapore-Australia service.
1943: Bombed and set on fire on April 14 at Milne Bay, New Guinea, with the loss of six lives; towed to Brisbane for repair.
1964: Sold in August to the Leung Yau Shipbuilding Co for £49,250 for scrap and broken up at Hong Kong.

CHARON
3,703 grt
1936: Caledon Shipbuilding & Engineering Co, Dundee, for the Ocean Stream Ship Co.
1964: Sold in May to Malayan Ship Breakers Ltd for £47,213 but re-sold by them to Chan Kai Kit, Panama, and renamed *Seng Kong No 1*.
1965: Sold for scrap to the Liam Bee Co in August and broken up at Singapore.

TELEMACHUS
9,061 grt
1939: Laid down by the Caledon Shipbuilding & Engineering Co, Dundee, for the Ocean Steam Ship Co. Requisitioned before completion by the Ministry of War Transport and renamed *Empire Activity*. Transferred to the Admiralty and completed as an aircraft carrier.
1942: Entered service as HMS *Activity*.
1946: Bought by Alfred Holt & Co in April, rebuilt as a merchant ship by Palmers Hebburn and assigned to the Glen Line as the *Breconshire*.
1967: Sold for scrap to Atak & Co Ltd, Osaka, and broken up at Kobe, never actually having sailed as a Blue Funnel ship.

JASON
6,310 grt
1939: Laid down by Cantieri Reunti dell Adriatico at Monfalcone as one of a series of ships for Lloyd Triestino. The owners being short of American currency and NSM "Oceaan" being one ship short of their normal six-ship fleet an agreement was reached whereby NSM "Oceaan" undertook to purchase one of the practically completed ships in return for payment in US dollars in New York.
1940: With the name "*Jason* Holland" painted in huge letters on her side the ship ran trials on May 10 under the Dutch flag and with a full Dutch crew and the NSM "Oceaan" acceptance party on board. The ship was complete in practically all respects except that she had no radio and it was not until she returned to Trieste in the evening that the Dutch personnel found that their country had been invaded that morning by German forces. An official of NSM "Oceaan" arrived in Trieste on May 11 with the Dutch registration documents but on May 14 the Italian authorities decided that the transfer of the *Jason* to Holland could not be allowed to take place. Instead she was placed with Societa Italiano di Armamento "Sidarma" and given the name *Sebastiano Veniero*. The Dutch personnel left Trieste on May 15 for Marseilles and were taken on by the *Perseus* to Liverpool where they arrived safely on June 13.
1941: Torpedoed on December 9 by HM submarines *Porpoise* and *Torbay* in the Mediterranean, five miles south of Navarino, Greece.

TELEMACHUS
8,265 grt
1943: Caledon Shipbuilding & Engineering Co, Dundee, for the Ocean Steam Ship Co.
1957: Transferred in October to the Glen Line and renamed *Monmouthshire*.
1963: Transferred to the Ocean Steam Ship Co and renamed *Glaucus*.
1964: Chartered by the China Navigation Co Ltd and renamed *Nanchang*.
1968: Sold for scrap at end of charter and broken up at Hong Kong by Leung Yau Shipbreakers.

PRIAM
9,795 grt
1939: Caledon Shipbuilding & Engineering Co, Dundee. Requisitioned by the Admiralty while still under construction with the intention of her being completed as an aircraft carrier but the work had progressed too far for this to be viable and she was finished according to the original specification.
1941: Entered service under the management of the Ocean Steam Ship Co.
1945: Reverted to full company ownership.
1948: Transferred to the Glen Line and renamed *Glenorchy*.
1970: Transferred to the Ocean Steam Ship Co and renamed *Phemius*.
1971: Sold for scrap and broken up in Taiwan.

Originally intended for the carriage of heavy supplies and locomotives to the Far East theatre of war, the "Rhexenor" did in fact carry locomotives on deck to Australia for the Government of Victoria. The arrangement of the masts, with one inside the funnel, is said to be unique

RHEXENOR
10,199 grt
1945: Laid down by the Caledon Shipbuilding & Engineering Co, Dundee, as one of the fast "Empire"-class for the Ministry of War Transport. Bought on the stocks by Alfred Holt & Co and completed to company requirements for the China Mutual Steam Navigation Co.
1975: Sold for scrap in May and renamed *Hexeno* (by removing the first and last letters of *Rhexenor*) for the delivery voyage to Kaohsiung, Taiwan, for demolition by the Shyeh Sheng Fuat Steel & Iron Works Co.

MEDON
7,376 grt
1942: Harland & Wolff, Belfast, as the *Empire Splendour* for the Ministry of War Transport (G. Heyn & Sons, managers).
1945: Management assigned in March to Alfred Holt & Co.
1946: Bought in June by Alfred Holt & Co and assigned to the Ocean Steam Ship Co as the *Medon*.
1963: Sold in January to Olistim Navigation Co Ltd, Monrovia, for £65,000 and renamed *Tina*.
1968: Sold to Sanspyridon Shipping Co, Cyprus (Olistim Navigation Co, managers).
1970: Sold for scrap and broken up at Shanghai.

STENTOR
10,203 grt
1946: Caledon Shipbuilding & Engineering Co, Dundee, for the Ocean Steam Ship Co, having been laid down as an "Empire"-class for the Ministry of War Transport.
1958: Transferred in November to the Glen Line and renamed *Glenshiel*.
1963: Transferred in January to the Ocean Steam Ship Co and renamed *Stentor*.
1973: Transferred to Elder Dempster without change of name.
1975: Sold for scrap in April and renamed *Tento* (by removing the first and last letters of *Stentor*) for the delivery voyage from Singapore to shipbreakers in Taiwan.

POLYDORUS
7,671 grt
1944: Permanente Metals Corporation, Richmond, California, as the *Salina Victory* for the United States Maritime Commission.
1946: Bought by Alfred Holt & Co and assigned to NSM "Oceaan" as the *Polydorus*.
1960: Transferred to Ocean Steam Ship Co and renamed *Talthybius*.
1971: Transferred to Elder Dempster without change of name but painted in Elder Dempster colours for service to West Africa. Sold for scrap in December to the Nan Feng Steel Enterprise Co and broken up at Taipei, Taiwan.

POLYPHEMUS
7,674 grt
1945: Permanente Metals Corporation, Richmond, California, as the *MacMurray Victory* for the United States Maritime Commission.
1946: Bought by Alfred Holt & Co and assigned to NSM "Oceaan" as the *Polyphemus*.
1960: Transferred in June to Ocean Steam Ship Co and renamed *Tantalus*.
1969: Laid-up in March in the River Fal. Bought later in the year by Reth Ym Nis & Kalundis, Panama, for scrap and renamed *Pelops* for the delivery voyage, with a cargo of scrap, to shipbreakers at Kaohsiung,

MEMNON
7,687 grt
1945: Permanente Metals Corporation, Richmond, California, as the *Phillips Victory* for the United States Maritime Commission.
1946: Bought by Alfred Holt & Co and assigned to the Ocean Steam Ship Co as the *Memnon*.
1957: Renamed *Glaucus*.
1962: Sold in September to the Ilium Steamship Co and renamed *Persian Ferdowsi*.
1965: Sold to Iranian Shipping Lines and renamed *Kashan*.
1966: Sold to P. J. Franoulis and A. & I. Cliafas, Piraeus, and renamed *Eleni K.*
1968: Sold to Iranian buyers and renamed *Pirouzi*.
1969: Arrived at Hong Kong in June being towed by the Japanese tug *Amaryllis* and was broken up.

MARON
7,688 grt
1945: Permanente Metals Corporation, Richmond, California, as the *Berwyn Victory* for the United States Maritime Commission.
1947: Bought by Alfred Holt & Co and assigned to the China Mutual Steam Navigation Co as the *Maron*.
1957: Renamed *Rhesus*.
1960: Laid-up in November in the River Fal.
1962: Sold in October to the Overseas Maritime Co Ltd, Monrovia, and renamed *Pacific Telstar*.
1974: Arrived at Kaohsiung in February for breaking-up by the China Steel Corporation.

MENTOR
7,642 grt
1945: Permanente Metals Corporation, Richmond, California, as the *Carthage Victory* for the United States Maritime Commission.
1947: Bought by Alfred Holt & Co and assigned to the Ocean Steam Ship Co as the *Mentor*.
1967: Sold to Lilly Navigation Ltd, Monrovia, and renamed *Mentora*.
1968: Sold to Western Star Steamship Co, Panama, and renamed *Vita*.
1969: Sold to Cullum Cia Nav SA, Panama, and renamed *Viva*.
1971: Renamed *Syra* for delivery voyage to Split, Yugoslavia, where she was broken up.

MYRMIDON
7,715 grt
1945: Permanente Metals Corporation, Richmond, California, as the *Ripon Victory* for the United States Maritime Commission.
1947: Bought by Alfred Holt & Co and assigned to the China Mutual Steam Navigation Co as the *Myrmidon*.
1971: Sold in September to Taiwanese interests for breaking-up and transferred to Elder Dempster Lines for the delivery voyage to the Tien Cheng Steel Manufacturing Co, Taipei.

EUMAEUS
7,308 grt
1943: Bethlehem Fairfield Shipyard Inc, Baltimore, as the *Simon B. Elliott* for the United States Maritime Commission but completed as the *Samnesse* for the Ministry of War Transport (Alfred Holt & Co, managers).
1947: Bought by Alfred Holt & Co and assigned to the China Mutual Steam Navigation Co as the *Eumaeus*.
1952: Transferred in March to the Glen Line and renamed *Glenshiel*.
1957: Transferred in July to the China Mutual Steam Navigation Co and renamed *Euryades*.
1961: Sold in March to Bounty Shipping Co Ltd, Hong Kong, for £120,000 and renamed *Marine Bounty*.
1966: Stranded off Hasieshan, China, on February 25 while bound from Chingwantao to Singapore with a cargo of coal. Refloated but driven ashore again and broke in two after being abandoned as a total loss.

EURYMEDON
7,314 grt
1943: Bethlehem Fairfield Shipyard Inc, Baltimore, as the *Matthew Brush* for the United States Maritime Commission but completed as the *Samoa* for the Ministry of War Transport (Alfred Holt & Co, managers).
1947: Bought by Alfred Holt & Co and assigned to the China Mutual Steam Navigation Co as the *Eurymedon*.
1952: Transferred in October to the Glen Line and renamed *Glenlogan*.
1957: Transferred in May to the China Mutual Steam Navigation Co and renamed *Eurymedon*.
1958: Sold to Etokila Compania Naviera SA, Panama, and renamed *Angelos* under Costa Rican flag.
1964: Sold to Michael A. Araktingi, Lebanon, and renamed *Mimosa*.
1966: Sold to Alplata Shipping Corporation, Monrovia, and renamed *Alplata*.
1967: Sold to Maria de Lourdes Shipping Co, Cyprus, and renamed *Anka*.
1971: Sold for scrap in June and broken up at Bilbao, Spain.

EURYPYLUS
7,292 grt
1943: Bethlehem Fairfield Shipyard Inc, Baltimore, as the *Augustine Herman* for the United States Maritime Commission but completed as the *Samsette* for the Ministry of War Transport (Alfred Holt & Co, managers).
1947: Bought in April by Alfred Holt & Co and assigned to the China Mutual Steam Navigation Co as the *Eurypylus*.
1950: Transferred in November to the Glen Line and renamed *Pembrokeshire*.
1957: Transferred in September to the China Mutual Steam Navigation Co and renamed *Eurypylus*.
1960: Sold in June to the Federal Shipping Co, Hong Kong, and renamed *Kota Bahru*.
1966: Sold to Cresta Shipping Co Inc, Panama, and renamed *Cresta*.
1968: Sold for scrap in February and broken up at Kaohsiung.

TALTHYBIUS
7,317 grt
1943: Bethlehem Fairfield Shipyard Inc, Baltimore, as the *Peter Cooper* for the United States Maritime Commission but completed as the
    Samarkand for the Ministry of War Transport (Alfred Holt & Co, managers).
1947: Bought in April by Alfred Holt & Co and assigned to the Ocean Steam Ship Co as the *Talthybius*
1954: Transferred in March to the Glen Line and renamed *Gleniffer.*
1958: Sold to the Colombine Shipping Co, Monrovia, and renamed *Dove.*
1965: Sold in December to the Patriarch Steamship Co, Monrovia, and renamed *Patraic Sky.*
1971: Sold for scrap and broken up at Split.

TANTALUS
7,297 grt
1943: Bethlehem Fairfield Shipyard Inc, Baltimore, as the *John T. Clark* for the United States Maritime Commission but completed as the
    Samcleve for the Ministry of War Transport (Alfred Holt & Co, managers).
1947: Bought in April by Alfred Holt & Co and assigned to the Ocean Steam Ship Co as the *Tantalus.*
1958: Sold in November to Luigi Pittaluga Vapori, Genoa, and renamed *Urbania.*
1965: Sold to Henry Coe & Clerici SpA, Genoa, and renamed *Cocler.*
1975: Sold for scrap in January to Italsider SpA and broken up at Vado, Italy.

TITAN
7,297 grt
1943: Bethlehem Fairfield Shipyard Inc, Baltimore, as the *James Carroll* for the United States Maritime Commission but completed as
    the *Samgara* for the Ministry of War Transport (Alfred Holt & Co, managers).
1947: Bought in April by Alfred Holt & Co and assigned to the Ocean Steam Ship Co as the *Titan.*
1950: Transferred in September to the Glen Line and renamed *Flintshire.*
1958: Transferred to the Ocean Steam Ship Co and renamed *Titan.*
1962: Sold in January to the Tidewater Commercial Co, Baltimore, for £92,500 and renamed *Titanus.*
1969: Sold for scrap and broken up at Mihara.

TROILUS
7,287 grt
1943: Bethlehem Fairfield Shipyard Inc, Baltimore, as the *Martin C. Thomas* for the United States Maritime Commission but completed
  as the *Samharle* for the Ministry of War Transport (Alfred Holt & Co, managers).
1947: Bought in April by Alfred Holt & Co and assigned to the Ocean Steam Ship Co as the *Troilus*.
1958: Sold in January to Cia de Navigacion San Agustin SA, Panama, and renamed *Green River* under Liberian registry.
1963: Sold for scrap and broken up at Osaka.

TYDEUS
7,234 grt
1944: Bethlehem Fairfield Shipyard Inc, Baltimore, as the *Samjack* for the Ministry of War Transport (Alfred Holt & Co, managers).
1947: Bought in April by Alfred Holt & Co and assigned to the Ocean Steam Ship Co as the *Tydeus*.
1950: Transferred in November to the Glen Line and renamed *Glenbeg*.
1958: Sold in April to the Forman Shipping & Trading Co, Panama, and renamed *Roan*.
1960: Sold to West African Carriers Corporation, Monrovia, and renamed *Jucar*.
1967: Sold for scrap in September and broken up at Mihara.

CALCHAS
8,298 grt
1947: Harland & Wolff, Belfast, for the Ocean Steam Ship Co.
1957: Transferred in December to the Glen Line and renamed *Glenfinlas.*
1962: Transferred in October to the Ocean Steam Ship Co and renamed *Calchas.*
1971: Transferred to Elder Dempster.
1972: Transferred to China Mutual Steam Navigation Co.
1973: Gutted by fire on July 22 off Port Kelang. Arrived under tow at Kaohsiung in October and was broken up by Kevn Hwa & Iron &
   Steel Works & Enterprise Co Ltd.

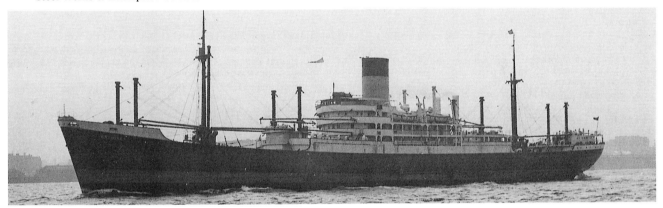

ANCHISES
8,292 grt
1947: Caledon Shipbuilding & Engineering Co, Dundee, for the Ocean Steam Ship Co.
1949: Bombed by Chinese Nationalist aircraft on June 21 while in the Whangpo River bound for Shanghai. Settled by the stern in shallow
   water with her engine-room flooded and passenger accommodation shattered. Attacked again, this time unsuccessfully, on the
   following day. After a hole 10ft by 6ft in the ship's side had been patched she was refloated and towed into Shanghai to discharge
   cargo. Subsequently towed to Kobe, Japan, for repair.
1973: Transferred in January to NMS "Oceaan" and renamed *Alcinous.*
1974: Transferred in August to the Glen Line and in November to the Ocean Steam Ship Co.
1975: Sold for scrap in September and broken up at Kaohsiung.

AENEAS
8,295 grt
1947: Caledon Shipbuilding & Engineering Co, Dundee, for the Ocean Steam Ship Co.
1972: Sold for scrap in April and broken up in Taiwan.

AGAPENOR
8,322 grt
1947: Scotts' Shipbuilding & Engineering Co, Greenock, for the China Mutual Steam Navigation Co.
1967: Trapped in the Great Bitter Lake on June 6 when the Suez Canal was closed as a result of hostilities between Israel and Egypt.
1968: Alfred Holt & Co gave notice to the insurers that they wished to abandon the ship but the offer was refused on the grounds that the company still had control of her.
1969: After lengthy negotiations the ship was declared a constructive total loss in February and was abandoned to the Liverpool & London War Risks Association in September, Alfred Holt & Co leaving a maintenance crew of seven on board.
1971: The ship was placed in the care of the nearby Czechoslovakian vessel *Lednice*.
1975: Sold by the War Risks Association in April to Grecomar Shipping Agency, Piraeus. Towed out of the canal on May 20 to Trieste for discharge of cargo.
1976: Sold to Faynar Shipping Co SA, Panama, and renamed *Nikos*.
1981: Sold for scrap and broken up by Ghulen Ali Kassim Ali & Co, Karachi.

ACHILLES
8,295 grt
1947: Caledon Shipbuilding & Engineering Co, Dundee, for the Ocean Steam Ship Co.
1949: Transferred in May to the Glen Line and renamed *Radnorshire*.
1962: Transferred in December to the China Mutual Steam Navigation Co and renamed *Asphalion*.
1966: Transferred in January to NSM "Oceaan" and renamed *Polyphemus*.
1972: Transferred in November to the China Mutual Steam Navigation Co and renamed *Asphalion*.
1975: Sold in October to Gulf (Shipowners) Ltd, London, and renamed *Gulf Anchor*.
1979: Sold for scrap and broken up at Kaohsiung.

ASTYANAX
8,319 grt
1948: Scotts' Shipbuilding & Engineering Co, Greenock, for the China Mutual Steam Navigation Co.
1957: Transferred in November to the Glen Line and renamed *Glenfruin*.
1962: Transferred in September to the China Mutual Steam Navigation Co and renamed *Astyanax*.
1972: Sold in December to Chun Yuan Steel Inc, Taipei, and broken up at Kaohsiung.

CLYTONEUS
8,214 grt
1948: Caledon Shipbuilding & Engineering Co, Dundee, for the Ocean Steam Shipb Co.
1971: Transferred to Elder Dempster Lines without change of name but painted in EDL colours.
1972: Sold for scrap in June and broken up at Kaohsiung by the Tong Yung Copper & Iron Co.

CYCLOPS
8,231 grt
1948: Scotts' Shipbuilding & Engineering Co, Greenock, for the Ocean Steam Ship Co.
1975: Renamed *Automedon* in July and transferred to Elder Dempster Lines in December without change of name but painted in EDL colours.
1977: After three months on charter to the Nigerian National Line, sold for scrap in August and broken up at Dalmuir by W. H. Arnott Young & Co.

DARDANUS
9,503 grt
1920: Harland & Wolff, Glasgow, for the Glen Line as the *Glenapp*.
1949: Transferred to the Ocean Steam Ship Co and renamed *Dardanus*.
1957: Sold for scrap in July and broken up at Inverkeithing by T. W. Ward & Co.

DOLIUS
9,460 grt
1922: Harland & Wolff, Glasgow, for the Glen Line as the *Glengarry*.
1939: Renamed *Glenstrae*.
1940: Bombed at London on September 7 and repaired.
1949: Transferred in February to the Ocean Steam Ship Co and renamed *Dolius*.
1952: Struck the wall while leaving Gladstone Dock, Liverpool, in July (the engines were put astern instead of ahead) and was not considered worth repairing. Sold for scrap the following month and broken up by T. W. Ward at Briton Ferry.

DEUCALION
9,513 grt
1920: Harland & Wolff, Glasgow, for the Glen Line as the *Glenogle*.
1949: Transferred to the Ocean Steam Ship Co and renamed *Deucalion*.
1956: Sold for scrap in March and broken up by T. W. Ward at Briton Ferry.

DYMAS
9,461 grt
1922: Harland & Wolff, Glasgow, for the Glen Line as the *Glenbeg*.
1949: Transferred in August to the Ocean Steam Ship Co and renamed *Dymas*.
1954: Sold for scrap in April and broken up by W. H. Arnot Young & Co at Dalmuir.

PELEUS
10,093 grt
1949: Cammell Laird & Co, Birkenhead, for the Ocean Steam Ship Co.
1972: Sold for scrap in February and broken up in Taiwan.

ANTILOCHUS
8,238 grt
1949: Harland & Wolff, Belfast, for the Ocean Steam Ship Co.
1975: Transferred in May to Elder Dempster Lines, same name but painted in EDL colours.
1976: Sold in November to Gulf (Shipowners) Ltd, London, for £242,500 and renamed *Gulf Orient*.
1978: Sold for scrap in June and broken up by Al Noor Steel Ltd, Gadani Beach, Karachi.

AUTOLYCUS
8,236 grt
1949: Vickers-Armstrongs Ltd, Newcastle, for the China Mutual Steam Navigation Co.
1974: Transferred in November to Elder Dempster Lines, same name but painted in EDL colours.
1975: Chartered in October by Nigerian National Line.
1976: Sold in February to Gulf Shipping Lines, London, and renamed *Gulf Trader*.
1978: Sold for scrap in April and broken up by Non Feng Steel Enterprises Co in Taiwan.

PYRRHUS
10,093 grt
1949: Cammell Laird & Co, Birkenhead, for the Ocean Steam Ship Co.
1964: Suffered a severe fire on November 16-17 while in Huskisson Dock, Liverpool.
1972: Sold for scrap in September and broken up by the Chin Tai Steel Enterprise Co in Taiwan.

ULYSSES
8,976 grt
1949: Joseph L. Thompson & Sons, Sunderland, for the Silver Line as the *Silverholly*. Bought by Alfred Holt & Co before completion
      and assigned to the China Mutual Steam Navigation Co as the *Ulysses*.
1971: Sold to N.D. Papalios Aegis Group and renamed *Aegis Saga* under the Cypriot flag.
1974: Sold for scrap and broken up at Shanghai.

AUTOMEDON
8,236 grt
1949: Vickers-Armstrongs Ltd, Newcastle, for the Ocean Steam Ship Co.
1971: Involved in a collison on December 17 with the Greek ship *San George* in the River Scheldt. Sold for scrap but repaired to seaworthy
      condition for voyage to Taiwan.
1972: Arrived at Kaohsiung in March for demolition.

LAERTES
8,270 grt
1949: Vickers-Armstrongs Ltd, Newcastle, for NSM "Oceaan".
1972: Transferred in March to Elder Dempster Lines, retaining Dutch flag. Transferred in August to the China Mutual Steam Navigation Co and renamed *Idomeneus* under British flag.
1975: Chartered variously to Elder Dempster Lines and Nigerian National Line.
1976: Sold in June to Gulf Lines, London, and renamed *Gulf Voyager*.
1978: Sold for scrap to Al Noor Steel Ltd and arrived at Gadani Beach in May for demolition.

HELENUS
10,125 grt
1949: Harland & Wolff, Belfast, for the Ocean Steam Ship Co.
1972: Sold for scrap in July and broken up at Kaohsiung.

PATROCLUS
10,109 grt
1950: Vickers-Armstrongs Ltd, Newcastle, for the China Mutual Steam Navigation Co.
1972: Renamed *Philoctetes.*
1973: Sold in February to the Chai Tai Steel Enterprise Co for breaking up at Kaohsiung.

Following the sale of the "Nestor", 14,629 grt (1913-1950), the "Jason" became the largest ship in the fleet apart from the "Rhexenor" and "Stentor" which were not laid down as Holt ships. When she arrived at Liverpool in February, 1969, she brought to an end the Blue Funnel UK/Australia service

JASON
10,160 grt
1950: Swan, Hunter & Wigham Richardson Ltd, Wallsend, for the China Mutual Steam Navigation Co.
1972: Sold for scrap in May to Swie Horng Co and broken up at Kaohsiung.

HECTOR
10,125 grt
1950: Harland & Wolff, Belfast, for the Ocean Steam Ship Co.
1972: Sold for scrap in July to the Sing Cheng Yung Iron & Steel Co and broken up at Kaohsiung.

PERSEUS
10,109 grt
1950: Vickers-Armstrongs Ltd, Newcastle, for the China Mutual Steam Navigation Co.
1973: Sold for scrap in January to the Li Chong Steel & Iron Works and broken up at Kaohsiung.

BELLEROPHON
7.707 grt
1950: Caledon Shipbuilding & Engineering Co, Dundee, for the Ocean Steam Ship Co.
1957: Transferred in October to the Glen Line and renamed *Cardiganshire*.
1972: Transferred to the China Mutual Steam Navigation Co and renamed *Bellerophon*.
1975: Transferred to Elder Dempster Lines, same name but painted in EDL colours.
1976: Transferred to the China Mutual Steam Navigation Co; sold later in the year to Saudi European Line and renamed *Obhor*.
1978: Sold in September to the Modern Commercial Corporation and broken up at Gadani Beach.

TEIRESIAS
8,910 grt
1950: Joseph L. Thompson & Sons, Sunderland, for the Silver Line as the *Silverelm*. Bought by Alfred Holt & Co before completion and assigned to NSM "Oceaan" as the *Teiresias*.
1960: Transferred in June to the Ocean Steam Ship Co and renamed *Telemachus*.
1971: Sold to Aegis Group and renamed *Aegis Courage* under Cypriot flag.
1974: Sold for scrap in February and broken up in China.

TEUCER
8,922 grt
1950: Joseph L. Thompson & Sons, Sunderland, for the Silver Line as the *Silverlaurel*. Bought by Alfred Holt & Co before completio..
and assigned to NSM "Oceaan" as the *Teucer*.
1960: Transferred in August to the China Mutual Steam Navigation Co and renamed *Telamon*.
1971: Sold in December to Aegis Group and renamed *Aegis Epic* under Cypriot flag.
1972: Sold for scrap in May and broken up at Shanghai.

ASCANIUS
7,692 grt
1950: Harland & Wolff, Belfast, for the Ocean Steam Ship Co.
1972: Transferred to Elder Dempster Lines and renamed *Akosombo*.
1973: Transferred to the China Mutual Steam Navigation Co and renamed *Ascanius*.
1976: Sold to Saudi Europe Line, Jeddah, and renamed *Mastura*.
1978: Sold for scrap in April and broken up by Hughes Bolckow Ltd at Blyth.

IXION
10,125 grt
1951: Harland & Wolff, Belfast, for the Ocean Steam Ship Co.
1972: Sold for scrap to Salvamiento y Demolici SA and broken up at Villaneuva y Geltru, Spain.

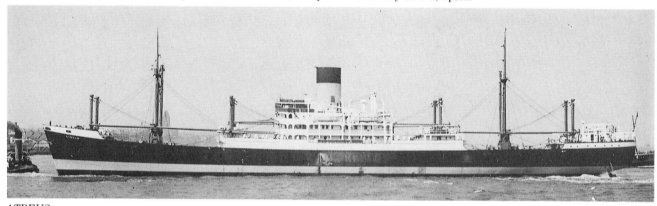

ATREUS
7,800 grt
1951: Vickers-Armstrongs Ltd, Newcastle, for the China Mutual Steam Navigation Co.
1977: Transferred in August to Elder Dempster Lines, sold in November to the Sherwood Shipping Co, Monrovia, and renamed *United Valiant* under the Singapore flag.
1979: Sold in February to the Tung Ho Steel Enterprise Corporation and broken up at Kaohsiung.

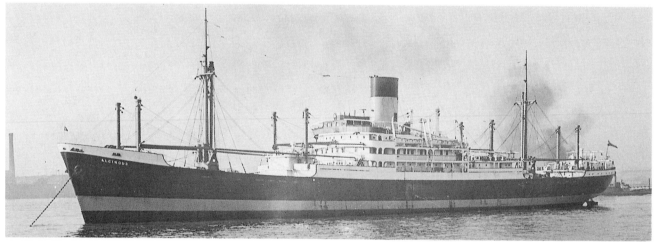

ALCINOUS
7,799 grt
1952: Vickers-Armstrongs Ltd, Newcastle, for the Ocean Steam Ship Co and originally intended to be named *Cadmus.*
1961: Transferred in January to NSM "Oceaan" and renamed *Polydorus.*
1973: Transferred in November to the China Mutual Steam Navigation Co.
1976: Sold in April to S.H. Alatas & Co, Jeddah, and renamed *Johara* but bought back in November, assigned to the Ocean Steam Ship Co and renamed *Polydorus.*
1977: Sold in November to the Hesperus Navigation Corporation, Monrovia, and renamed *Matina* under the Panamanian flag.
1978: Sold for scrap in April and broken up at Gadani Beach.

The "Nestor" was one of the first examples of a merchant ship running at very high engine temperature and pressure conditions. She steamed at 625 lb/sq in pressure in watertube boilers at a final temperature of 950°F and, like many other Holt vessels, marked an important development in the history of marine engineering

NESTOR
7,802 grt
1952: Caledon Shipbuilding & Engineering Co, Dundee, for the Ocean Steam Ship Co.
1968: Transferred in December to the Glen Line and renamed *Glenaffaric*.
1970: Transferred to the Ocean Steam Ship Co and renamed *Orestes*.
1971: Sold to Aegis Group and renamed *Aegis Dignity* under the Cypriot flag.
1973: Sold for scrap in November and broken up at Shanghai.

NELEUS
7,802 grt
1953: Caledon Shipbuilding & Engineering Co, Dundee, for the China Mutual Steam Navigation Co.
1971: Sold to Aegis Group and renamed *Aegis Fable*.
1972: Transferred within the group and renamed *Aegis Trust*.
1974: Sold for scrap in March and broken up at Shanghai.

LAOMEDON
7.864 grt
1953: Vickers-Armstrongs Ltd, Newcastle, for the China Mutual Steam Navigation Co and originally intended to be named *Admetus*.
1977: Sold in March to the Regent Navigation Corporation, Monrovia, and renamed *Aspasia* under the Panamanian flag.
1978: Sold for scrap and broken up at Gadani Beach.

EUMAEUS
7,869 grt
1953: Caledon Shipbuilding & Engineering Co, Dundee, for the Ocean Steam Ship Co and originally intended to be named *Cadmus*.
1962: Transferred in August to NSM "Oceaan".
1978: Sold in February to the Hai Kwang Enterprise Corporation and broken up at Kaohsiung.

ADRASTUS
7,859 grt
1953: Vickers-Armstrongs Ltd, Newcastle, for the Ocean Steam Ship Co.
1960: Transferred in August to NSM "Oceaan".
1975: Transferred in November to Elder Dempster Lines, same name but funnel painted in EDL colours.
1978: Sold in February to the Rhodeswell Shipping Co SA, Limasol, and renamed Anassa.
1981: Sold in December and broken up at Gadani Beach.

ELPENOR
7,757 grt
1954: Harland & Wolff, Belfast, for the China Mutual Steam Navigation Co.
1976: Transferred in November to Elder Dempster Lines.
1977: Sold in June to Cremorne Bay Shipping, Liberia, and renamed United Concorde under Panamanian flag.
1979: Sold in August to the Chang Iron & Steel Works and broken up in Taiwan.

LYCAON
7,859 grt
1954: Vickers-Armstrongs Ltd, Newcastle, for the China Mutual Steam Navigation Co.
1960: Transferred in November to NSM "Oceaan".
1974: Transferred to Ocean Steam Ship Co.
1975: Transferred in July to Elder Dempster Lines, same name but painted in EDL colours.
1976: Transferred in December to the China Mutual Steam Navigation Co and renamed *Glaucus.*
1977: Sold in March to Marlborough Maritime Inc, Monrovia, and renamed *United Vanguard* under the Singapore flag.
1979: Suffered an engine failure on May 12 following the fracture of a sea water cooling pipe while bound from Sharjah to Bassein. The ship was abandoned in rough seas with the loss of one life and was last sighted listing badly on May 22.

THESEUS
7,804 grt
1955: Caledon Shipbuilding & Engineering Co, Dundee, for the Ocean Steam Ship Co. (The ship was named on October 12, 1954, but could not be launched because of a shipyard strike. She finally took the water without ceremony on November 10).
1971: Sold in June to Aegis Group and renamed *Aegis Myth* under the Cypriot flag.
1972: Transferred within the group and renamed *Aegis Care.*
1973: Sold for scrap in November and broken up at Shanghai.

DEMODOCUS
7,968 grt
1955: Vickers-Armstrongs Ltd, Newcastle, for the Ocean Steam Ship Co.
1970: Transferred in June to the Glen Line and renamed *Glenroy*.
1972: Transferred in April to the Ocean Steam Ship Co and renamed *Demodocus*.
1973: Sold in April to the Nan Yang Shipping Co, Macao, and renamed *Hongsia*.
1979: Sold to the Chinese Bureau of Maritime Transport Administration and renamed *Hong Qi 137*.

DIOMED
7,984 grt
1956: Caledon Shipbuilding & Engineering Co, Dundee, for the China Mutual Steam Navigation Co.
1970: Transferred in June to the Glen Line and renamed *Glenbeg*.
1972: Transferred in June to the Ocean Steam Ship Co and renamed *Diomed*.
1973: Sold in February to the Nan Yang Shipping Co, Macao, and renamed *Kaising* under the Somali flag.
1983: Sold for scrap and broken up at Kaohsiung.

DOLIUS
7,964 grt
1956: Harland & Wolff, Belfast, for the Ocean Steam Ship Co.
1970: Transferred in November to the Glen Line and renamed *Glenfruin*.
1972: Transferred in May to the Ocean Steam Ship Co and renamed *Dolius*. Sold the following November to the Nan Yang Shipping Co, Macao, and renamed *Hung Nien* under the Somali flag.
1977: Sold to the Chinese Bureau of Maritime Transportation and renamed *Hong Qi 119*.
1984: Renamed *Zhan Dou 51*.

ANTENOR
7,974 grt
1957: Vickers-Armstrongs (Shipbuilders) Ltd, Newcastle, for the Ocean Steam Ship Co.
1970: Transferred in November to the Glen Line and renamed *Glenlochy*.
1972: Transferred in June to the Ocean Steam Ship Co and renamed *Dymas*.
1973: Sold in April to the Nan Yang Shipping Co, Macao, and renamed *Kaiyun* under the Somali flag.
1976: Sold to the High Seas Navigation Corporation SA, Panama.

ACHILLES
7,974 grt
1957: Vickers-Armstrongs (Shipbuilders) Ltd, Newcastle, for the Ocean Steam Ship Co.
1972: Transferred in May to the China Mutual Steam Navigation Co and renamed *Dardanus*.
1973: Sold in April to the Nan Yang Shipping Co, Macao, and renamed *Kiago* under the Somali flag.
1977: Sold to the High Seas Navigation Corporation SA, Panama.
1982: Arrived at Calcutta in June for demolition.

MENELAUS
8,539 grt
1957: Caledon Shipbuilding & Engineering Co, Dundee, for the Ocean Steam Ship Co.
1972: Transferred to Elder Dempster Lines and renamed *Mano*.
1977: Renamed *Oti*.
1978: Sold in May to Thenamaris Maritime Inc, Piraeus, and renamed *El Star* under the Cypriot flag.
1979: Sold for scrap in February to Dong Kuk Steel Co and broken up at Busan, South Korea.

MENESTHEUS
8,510 grt
1958: Caledon Shipbuilding & Engineering Co, Dundee, for the Ocean Steam Ship Co.
1977: Transferred in July to Elder Dempster Lines and renamed *Onitsha*.
1978: Sold in May to Thenamaris Maritime Inc, Piraeus, for £148,000 and renamed *El Island* under the Cypriot flag.
1979: Sold in March to the Lung Fa Steel & Iron Co and broken up at Kaohsiung.

AJAX
7,974 grt
1958: Vickers-Armstrongs (Shipbuilders) Ltd, Newcastle, for the China Mutual Steam Navigation Co.
1972: Renamed *Deucalion*.
1973: Sold in February to the Brilliance Steamship Co (Nan Yang Shipping Co, Macao) and renamed *Kailok*.
1982: Sold for scrap and broken up in Taiwan.

GUNUNG DJATI

17,891 grt

1936: Blohm & Voss, Hamburg, for the German East Africa Line as the *Pretoria*.

1939-45: Accommodation ship for the German Navy and hospital ship.

1945: Captured in May by British forces and taken over by the Ministry of War Transport as the troopship *Empire Doon* under the management of the Orient Line.

1949: Renamed *Empire Orwell* after a £2mn refit.

1958: Chartered to the Pan Islamic Steamship Co, Karachi, for the carriage of Moslem pilgrims to and from Mecca via Jeddah. At the end of her first season (November) she was bought by Alfred Holt & Co for the same purpose and assigned to the Ocean Steam Ship Co as the *Gunung Djati*.

1959: Entered service in March after being refitted by Barclay, Curle & Co, Glasgow, for the carriage of 106 First-class pilgrims and 2,000 others.

1962: Sold in February for £585,000 to the Indonesian Government for the same purpose.

1977: Transferred to the Indonesian Navy as a troopship and renamed *Kri Tanjung Pandan*.

1987: Sold for scrap and broken up at Kaohsiung.

MACHAON

8,530 grt

1959: Caledon Shipbuilding & Engineering Co, Dundee, for the Ocean Steam Ship Co.

1970: Transferred to NSM "Oceaan".

1977: Transferred in August to Elder Dempster Lines and renamed *Obuasi*.

1978: Sold to Thenamaris Maritime Inc, Piraeus, for £187,000 and renamed *El Sea* under the Cypriot flag; sold again later in the year to Tartan Shipping Ltd, Monrovia, and renamed *Med Endeavour*.

1979: Sold to the Sing Cheng Yung Iron & Steel Co and broken up at Kaohsiung.

MEMNON
8,504 grt
1959: Vickers-Armstrongs (Shipbuilders) Ltd, Newcastle, for the China Mutual Steam Navigation Co.
1975: Renamed *Stentor.*
1977: Transferred in April to Elder Dempster Lines and renamed *Owerri.*
1978: Sold in May to Thenamaris Maritime Inc, Piraeus, for £172,000 and renamed *Europe.*
1982: Reported in July to be laid-up at Stylis.
1987: Transferred to Maltese flag and renamed *Primus.*
1988: Arrived India for demolition.

MELAMPUS
8,511 grt
1960: Vickers-Armstrongs (Shipbuilders) Ltd, Newcastle, for the Ocean Steam Ship Co.
1967: Trapped in the Great Bitter Lake on June 6 when the Suez Canal was closed as a result of hostilities between Israel and Egypt.
1968: Alfred Holt & Co gave notice to the insurers that they wished to abandon the ship but the offer was refused on the grounds that the company still had control of her.
1969: After lengthy negotiations the ship was declared a constructive total loss in February and was abandoned to the Liverpool & London War Risks Association in September, Alfred Holt & Co leaving a maintenance crew of seven on board.
1971: The ship was placed in the care of the nearby Czechoslovakian vessel *Lednice.*
1975: Sold by the War Risks Association to Grecomar Shipping Agency, Piraeus. Towed out of the canal on May 20 to Trieste for discharge of cargo.
1976: Renamed *Annoula II.*
1983: Sold for scrap and broken up at Karachi.

MARON
8,531 grt
1960: Caledon Shipbuilding & Engineering Co, Dundee, for the Ocean Steam Ship Co.
1975: Transferred to the China Mutual Steam Navigation Co and renamed *Rhexenor.*
1977: Transferred in July to Elder Dempster Lines and renamed *Opobo.*
1978: Sold in May to Thenamaris Marine Inc, Piraeus for £192,000 and renamed *El Fortune;* later operated by the Belton Shipping Corporation, Monrovia, and renamed *Europe II.*
1982: Laid-up at Piraeus.
1984: Sold to Trade Shipping Ltd, Malta.
1987: Sold for scrap and broken up at Aliaga, Turkey.

The first ship in the fleet to be built by John Brown & Co, the design of the "Centaur" called for a vessel which could accommodate 200 passengers along with 700 head of cattle or 4,500 sheep and sit on the bottom when the tide receded at certain Australian ports

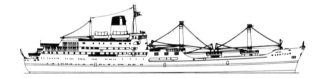

CENTAUR
7,988 grt
1964: John Brown & Co (Clydebank) Ltd, Glasgow, for the Ocean Steam Ship Co.
1967: Transferred to the China Mutual Steam Navigation Co.
1973: Transferred to Eastern Fleets Ltd, a member of the Alfred Holt group of companies, and registered in Singapore.
1978: Transferred to Blue Funnel (SEA) Pte Ltd, Singapore.
1982: Chartered by Curnow Shipping Ltd with an option to buy which was not taken up.
1986: Sold to China Ocean Shipping Co and renamed *Haida.*

PRIAM
12,094 grt
1966: Vickers Ltd, Newcastle, for the Ocean Steam Ship Co.
1972: Transferred to the China Mutual Steam Navigation Co.
1978: Sold to C.Y. Tung, Hong Kong, and renamed *Oriental Champion*.
1985: Sold for scrap and broken up at Kaohsiung.

PEISANDER
12,094 grt
1967: Vickers Ltd, Newcastle, for the Ocean Steam Ship Co.
1972: Transferred to the China Mutual Steam Navigation Co.
1978: Sold to C.Y. Tung, Hong Kong, and renamed *Oriental Exporter*.
1981: Renamed *Main Express*.
1984: Renamed *Oriental Exporter*.
1986: Sold for scrap and broken up at Kaohsiung.

PROTESILAUS
12,094 grt
1967: Vickers Ltd, Newcastle, for the Ocean Steam Ship Co.
1972: Transferred to the China Mutual Steam Navigation Co.
1978: Sold to C.Y. Tung, Hong Kong, and renamed *Oriental Importer*.
1985: Damaged by rocket attack in the Arabian Gulf on June 1; sold for scrap and broken up at Kaohsiung.

PROMETHEUS
12,094 grt
1967: Vickers Ltd, Newcastle, for the Ocean Steam Ship Co.
1972: Transferred to the China Mutual Steam Navigation Co.
1979: Sold to C.Y. Tung, Hong Kong, and renamed *Oriental Merchant*.
1980: Transferred within C.Y. Tung ownership and renamed *Oriental Merchant No 1,* later reverted to *Oriental Merchant*.
1984: Renamed *293*.
1986: Sold for scrap and broken up at Kaohsiung.

SARPEDON
8,790 grt
1939: Nederlandsche Scheepvaarts Maats, Amsterdam, for the Glen Line as the *Denbighshire*.
1967: Transferred to the China Mutual Steam Navigation Co and renamed *Sarpedon*.
1968: Transferred to the Ocean Steam Ship Co.
1969: Sold for scrap and broken up at Kaohsiung.

DARDANUS
9,677 grt
1940: Burmeister & Wain, Copenhagen, for the Glen Line as the *Glengarry*. Captured by German forces and renamed *Meersburg* for operation as a U-boat depot ship by the Hamburg-Amerika Line.
1942: Conversion to an armed merchant cruiser started in Holland.
1945: Commissioned into the German Navy as the *Hansa*. Recaptured by British forces in May and placed under the Ministry of War Transport as the *Empire Humber*.
1946: Sold to Alfred Holt & Co and assigned to the Glen Line as the *Glengarry*.
1970: Transferred to the Ocean Steam Ship Co and renamed *Dardanus*.
1971: Transferred to the Glen Line while at sea and renamed *Glengarry* for the delivery voyage to breakers at Sakaide, Japan, but the change could not be put into physical effect and she arrived with "Dardanus" still on her hull.

PHRONTIS
12,299 grt
1967: Mitsubishi Heavy Industries, Nagasaki, for the Glen Line as the *Pembrokeshire.*
1972: Transferred briefly to the Ocean Steam Ship Co and renamed *Phrontis* and then to the China Mutual Steam Navigation Co.
1982: Sold to Gulf Shipping Lines, London, and renamed *Gulf Osprey.*
1983: Sold to Iran Shipping Lines and renamed *Iran Ejtehad.*
Pictured while on charter to Swedish East Asiatic Line

PHEMIUS
12,094 grt
1967: John Brown & Co (Clydebank) Ltd, Glasgow, for the Glen Line as the *Glenfinlas.*
1972: Transferred to the China Mutual Steam Navigation Co and renamed *Phemius.*
1978: Sold to the China Navigation Co and renamed *Kweichow.*
1983: Sold to the Saudi Venture Corporation, Jeddah, and renamed *Saudi Kawther.*

PATROCLUS
12,299 grt
1966: Mitsubishi Heavy Industries, Nagasaki, for the Glen Line as the *Glenalmond*.
1973: Transferred to the China Mutual Steam Navigation Co and renamed *Patroclus*.
1977: Transferred to NSM "Oceaan".
1978: Transferred to the China Mutual Steam Navigation Co.
1982: Sold to Rajab & Co, Jeddah, and renamed *Rajab 1*.
1984: Sold to the Molasses Trading & Export Co at Port Rashid after being on fire on July 18. Renamed *Sahar* for voyage to breakers at Gadani Beach.

PERSEUS
12,089 grt
1967: Vickers Ltd, Newcastle, for the Glen Line as the *Radnorshire*.
1973: Transferred to the China Mutual Steam Navigation Co and renamed *Perseus*.
1978: Sold to the China Navigation Co and renamed *Kwangsi*.
1982: Renamed *Asia Dragon*.
1983: Sold to the Saudi Venture Corporation, Jeddah, and renamed *Saudi Zam Zam*.